SITA'S CHOICE

SITA'S CHOICE

Poems by

ATHENA KASHYAP

STEPHEN F. AUSTIN STATE UNIVERSITY PRESS

Stephen F. Austin State University Press
P.O. Box 13007, SFA Station
Nacogdoches, TX 75962-3007
sfapress@sfasu.edu

LIBRARY OF CONGRESS IN PUBLICATION DATA
Kashyap, Athena.
Sita's Choice/ Athena Kashyap

p. cm.
ISBN: 978-1-62288-905-1

1. Poetry. 2. Indian Poetry. 3. Kashyap, Athena.

PRAISE FOR SITA'S CHOICE

Athena Kashyap's poems are alive and supple paeans to life, celebrating the aches and wisdoms of the human body as well as a sensuous, feral womanhood. Sita as fecund earth goddess and the wronged woman of Indian myth is the metaphor that surfaces time and again through these poems. This metaphor is most fully realized, to my mind, in the poems that sing with lyrical abandon of love, longing, and motherhood. Erotic, ripe, succulent with desire, these tributes to the "formless, uncharted shape of love," its shape-shifting surprises, its exultation, and the pervasive mystery of pain, "multi-hued, magnificent."

 —Arundhati Subramanium
 poet, author of *When God is a Traveler* (2014)

In her second book of poems, *Sita's Choice*, Athena Kashyap takes on many of the familiar Indian myths, and reinterprets and contextualizes them in a contemporary way. There is lyricism, questioning, pleading, worship, evocation and watercolor-like painting of scenes with words. There is also a beautiful clash and confluence of tradition in this book– all felt intensely with oblique vividness.

 —Sudeep Sen, poet
 author of *Aria* (2011) and other books

Athena Kashyap's *Sita's Choice* is a revelation. These "Sitas" and their sisters moan, sigh, and dance their way through ravaged ecosystems, trailing sacrifice and sensuality, holding out the possibility of hope as they go about their daily work— "rebirthing forests, rewriting the stories."

 —Minal Hajratwallah
 author of *Leaving India: My Family's Journey from Five Valleys to Five Continents*

for Ishwar, Ishika & Anika

ACKNOWLEDGEMENTS

Poems in this collection, sometimes in different versions, have been published in *Prairie Schooner, Quiddity, Sugar Mule, Vaani, The Missing Slate, All Roads Will Lead You Home* and other journals. They have also appeared in the anthologies: *Modern English Poetry*, edited by Sudeep Sen (forthcoming), and *Red Sky: Poetry on the Global Epidemic of Violence Against Women*, published by Sable Books (2016).

The poem, "Shame" has lines from the song, *Mere Sapno ki Rani*, lyrics by Anand Bakshi, for the film Aradhana (1969); "Tatiana" has lines from William Blake's "The Tyger" (1794).

Special thanks to Manisha Jha Mishra, national awardee in Mithila Painting, and founder of the Madhubani Art Center, for allowing me to use the image of her painting, *Sita*, which she painted especially for the book. Lisa Stonestreet, Melissa Chianta, Rima Kashyap, Tanu Mehrotra, and Ishwar Parulkar helped with the editing and copyediting of the manuscript.

Many friends, fellow poets, and mentors took the time to review the manuscript over the years. Thanks to Tanu Mehrotra Wakefield, Sarah Bardeen, Sudeep Sen, Arundhati Subramanium, Minal Hajratwallah, Steven Shroeder, Vivek Narayanan, Priya Sarukkai Chabria, Indu Krishnan, Geeta Rao, and Philip Nikolayev for their valuable feedback. Special thanks to Tanu for her thorough reading and insights which helped shaped the manuscript in its final stages.

Kimberly Verhines from Stephen F. Austin State University Press has been a great support. I thank her for continuing to believe in my work, for her patience, and also for accomodating my many requests. I appreciate the freedom and trust she puts in me in all stages of production.

Thanks to all my family, including Kunal, Raena, Madhavi Parulkar, and especially my mother, Rima. Lastly, my dearest Ishwar, Ishika, and Anika give me strength and purpose day after day. I thank them for allowing me to pursue my passions, even though I sometimes may ignore them while I am doing so. I could not write without their love and support.

FOREWORD

In this collection of linked poems, I use the lens of Sita, from the epic *Ramayana*, to explore issues facing women living in contemporary India. While most Indians will understand the context of these poems, Western readers might need more of an introduction. I have also included a notes section and glossary of Indian words at the end of the book.

The poet Valmiki composed the *Ramayana* in Sanskrit around 300 BCE. Since then, there have been numerous versions based upon his writing. The epic recounts the life of Ram, crown prince of Ayodhya, who is also considered an *avatar* (earthly manifestation) of the great Hindu god, Vishnu. To fulfil a promise his father made to one of his wives, Ram was banished to the forest for fourteen years. His wife, Sita, and brother, Lakshman, chose to accompany him. As part of their travails in the forest, the brothers fought many demons and demonesses (*rakshasas* and *rakshasis*), including the *rakshasi,* Shurpanakha, whose romantic overtures both Ram and Laksman rejected, and whose nose Lakshman cut off when she attacked Sita. Shurpanakha fled to her brother Ravan, the ten-headed king of Lanka.

Promising revenge, Ravan, in the guise of a *sadhu* or holy man, managed to deceive Sita into leaving a protective line in the ground Lakshman had drawn around her hut (this event is not in Valmiki's version), and carried her away with him to Lanka. Ram and Lakshman set out to look for her, and by and by enlisted the help of the monkey god, Hanuman. Hanuman found Sita in Lanka, but he was captured soon afterwards. His tail was lit on fire, but he managed to escape and burned down most of Lanka. After he returned, Ram amassed a huge army of monkeys and crossed the Indian Ocean to attack Lanka. They were victorious, killing Ravan and defeating his army. They returned to Ayodhya as heroes.

To this day, Hindus all over the world celebrate Ram's return to Ayodhya at Diwali, the Indian New Year, by lighting firecrackers and lamps called *diyas*. Hindus worship Ram as the ideal son and model king who puts his duty to his father and his people above everything else. Likewise, many Hindu men and women consider Sita to be the ideal woman—a good mother who is submissive to her husband's needs.

This book of poems focuses on Sita's life and story, and the women of India, whom I refer to as Sita's daughters. Valmiki's *Ramayana* portrays Sita as a dutiful wife and mother but one who has little or no voice at all. Her suffering is notable especially when Ram rejects her after his people gossip about her stay in Ravan's palace. Ram publicly asks Sita to prove that her body has not been violated by Ravan. Sita performs *agni pariksha* or the fire test to show her purity, and jumps into a fire. Even though she comes out of the fire unscathed, the people of Ayodhya are not convinced, and Ram asks Lakshman to take Sita away and leave her in the forest. It is here that Sita, pregnant with Ram's twin boys, meets Valmiki who tutors her children and then writes the *Ramayana*. Many years later, Ram comes across his twin sons. While he willingly accepts them, he asks Sita to once again perform the fire test. This time, Sita refuses, and calls to her mother, Earth. The ground opens up, and the goddess Earth embraces Sita and takes her away.

The title of this poetry collection, *Sita's Choice*, refers to Sita's decision to leave Ram and return to the earth. This is a pro-active decision, markedly different from her otherwise submissive nature in Valmiki's *Ramayana*. I'm also interested in Sita's relationship to the soil—being the daughter of Earth; she can be viewed as a protector of the environment.

Sita's abandonment heralds the current mistreatment of women in India, which includes rape, dowry deaths, female foeticide. Through three main sections—body, seed, and soil—all of which are pertinent to Sita, I explore the relationship contemporary women have to their bodies, children, and the earth.

As pointed out earlier, Valmiki's *Ramayana* is just one of the many versions created over the years. While I have poems addressed to Valmiki in this book, I also refer to incidents that are mentioned in other versions. Keeping with the spirit of the *Ramayana*, a living, breathing story, I have also taken the liberty to embellish events and personalities differently than they are portrayed in Valmiki's *Ramayana*. These are purely fictional and poetic explorations, and should be read and interpreted as such.

Athena Kashyap

CONTENTS

INVOCATION TO GANESHA / 1

SITA SEPTET

SITA / 7

SITA IN DOMBIVLI / 8

PRIMETIME NEWS / 9

SITA'S CHOICE / 10

LETTER TO VALMIKI FROM THE OTHER SITA / 11

FIRE TRIALS / 14

DEAR SITA / 18

BODY

OFFERING / 21

HANDS LATTICED / 22

PUTTAMA'S MIRACLE WASH / 23

GALINA / 24

PORTRAIT /26

PUNJABI WEDDING / 27

SUMMONS / 29

AIR / 30

THE OTHER WIDOWS / 31

WHORLS / 32

BELOVED MUMTAZ / 33

BODY II: THE CITY IS CLAIMED

SUNDAY AFTERNOON STROLL / 37

RAILWAY STATION / 38

THE PAINTED LADY / 39

THE DOLL / 40

THE MIRROR / 41

HIJRA AT THE INTERSECTION / 42

CROCODILE LAKE REVISITED / 44

THIS CITY IS CLAIMED / 47

SHAME / 49

DEVIL'S DAUGHTERS / 51

CITY OF WIDOWS / 53

SEED

BLOOD, OIL, & WATER / 57

CONCRETE / 59

FIRST TRIMESTER / 60

FRUITS

    Santra (orange) / 61

    Anjeer (fig) / 61

    Aam (mango) / 62

RAIN DANCE

    Potter / 63

    Spring / 63

    Woman / 64

    Pain / 65

    Drum / 65

Geometry / 65

Journey / 66

Baby Krishna / 66

Oceans / 67

Words / 67

SLEEP SONATAS / 68

THE FIRST YEAR / 69

ORBIT / 70

PUBERTY / 71

SOIL

EVOLUTION / 75

BACK TO THE WOMB / 76

OMENS / 77

THE TOY ROOM / 79

TATIANA / 80

M.S. ATTACK / 81

THE LEELA POEMS

Independence day / 84

Boats / 85

Indulgence / 86

Blessings / 86

Blood bond / 87

Badmaash / 87

Aai / 88

Lemon rice / 89

Leela's song / 89

NOTES / 91

GLOSSARY / 93

INVOCATION TO GANESHA

The elephant crosses the road,
stops to ponder and stare,
looking down at us
from his enormous pedestal.

What he sees with his mind's eye,
I will never know. Vast plains
surround us—a sea where he is
buoyant, while we flounder—

trying to clutch at his dancing trunk,
breathe the fragrance of the universe.

And the Earth, which had given Sita birth, yawned and took back her suffering child into her bosom.

-Ramayana, Book 12
(Translated by R.C. Dutta)

SITA SEPTET

SITA

Hazara Rama temple, Hampi, India

springs out of stone
pillars that tell us
the story of her life
through carvings
that speak louder
than she ever did.
Leads my two girls and me
into her innermost
sanctum—a deep
crack in the ground.
Don't be afraid, she says,
fall inside with me,
find our cut-off
tongues
grown into huge trees—
leaves fluttering
our myriad,
unsaid thoughts.

SITA IN DOMBIVLI

On dark nights,
her husband's back—
cold and hard

the trains' relentless clatter,
spewing out crowds,
grime that makes its way

into her tiny house she scrubs
to keep the curtains white,
floors gleaming.

No rest—one more *phulka*
to balloon, one more
tear to mend.

Through the grills, she sees
a train's blazing light
cleave the darkness.

She runs outside, hops
on board, her life suddenly
open to multiple tracks.

Gone—her departure
wakes up the world
and her sleeping husband.

PRIMETIME NEWS

July 13, 2012, Guwahati, Assam

Not allowed   to forget
she sees   again   and again
Hydra hands   tearing off
her panties   her shirt
black horizontal bar across
her buttocks   and breasts
her   only   cover.

Close up   her face   dissolves
into   blank   squares.
She does   not   know
who   she   is anymore.
She clutches   at   the remote
but   cannot   stop
Ravan's hundredthousandeyes
from devouring her.

SITA'S CHOICE

In response to a painting, Sita Taken by Goddess Earth,
by Raja Ravi Verma

Led to the edge of the picture frame
towards a yawning hole in the ground

Sita cannot hide the dismay that drips
from her eyes. Integrity intact, she holds up

her *pallav*, flailing from false accusations.
Pink and gold no longer unite

and in the widening gap
between Ram and herself—

a single mother's ascetic years
lost among hermits and trees

in contrast to the fierce glitter of gold,
rush to clutch the sword.

In the gap too, Ram's shoes—
shucked off like his responsibility to Sita.

Still, he questions Sita's choice
to return to her mother, Earth,

who leads Sita away, arms clasped
around her waist, fingers locked,

his own palm hanging above the crack—
open and empty.

LETTER TO VALMIKI
FROM THE OTHER SITA

You knew me well,
dear Valmiki,
how could you forget—

I loved to rake mud
with my nails,
burst into the palace,
a spring in spate,
full of bark and dirt,
yet to be tamed by Shiva's coils
or your pen.
Junglee girl you used to call me
affectionately, but not without
a hint of admonition.

The oscillations Ram twanged
with my bow—O shivers!
Drove me to choose him,
grow the resonance.
I'm sure you recall
I was first to push
for the forest—
fourteen years of twigs
crackling beneath bare feet
to stoke our fires.

Knowing well my propensity
to cross lines, especially
those drawn to contain me,
my occasional *junglee* ways,
days when I felt like
tearing out my hair
as a single mother in the forest,
wished for girls—
you still chose to write me
pure as a lit pyre,
dead wood good only
to jump into the fire
just to prove a point, or else
disappear into the ground.

Ram never could stand
another man's eyes on me,
let alone ten pairs
but he fought his demons
(and Ravan's army) in Lanka,
and won. But how to convince
his subjects, the residents of Ayodhya,
no other man had touched me?
Flames turning into flowers
on touching my body
was a nice touch, dear Valmiki,
but not enough.

It broke my heart,
but the ground,
the story, as you told it,
was flimsy, bound

to give way any day.
I had to leave—get back
to my mother's house
while I still had fire,
revive body and mind
lost in the fanciful
flourishes of your pen,
feel the earth,
supple and pliant
with bare hands,
let loose my tongue,
let my fingers run
with ink and mud.

FIRE TRIALS

I.
The immodesty—
arriving at her husband's house
with light suitcases.

> Her father's life—
> mortgaged to pay
> for her wedding

nothing more left
to give. No choice for her
but to redeem herself

> in the "accidental"
> kitchen fire set-off
> with a little help

from her husband,
in-laws, and the kerosene
from the stove.

> Dragged. Doused.
> *Sari* set alight.
> Fire whirling

her burning body
into a swirling
Diwali *chakra.*

> No Sita she was—
> burnt to a crisp
> Damned.

II.
In this city that shrinks
the dicks of poor villagers
like him—

the enormous bus he drove
that night with friends
roaring so loud
the English speaking, jean-
wearing, boyfriend toting
girl who got on the bus
talking too loud.
Shut her up,
put her in her place.
Lunds suddenly large,
grown longer
with an iron rod
Jam her, ram her.
throw her, along with
her boyfriend—out of the bus,
bloodied intestines
trailing behind.
Roar away.

III.
Docile, doe-eyed
bride turned
rakshasi

attacking his manhood
daring to earn
as much and more than him—
her *pati-dev*,
peeling away his divinity
making him
less than him.
He slices off her nose
with a kitchen knife

15

exposes her for who
she really is—
Shurpanakha.

IV.
Breath beating at her
heart so hard
running more

        naked than naked
        down village paths
        she knows so well

but does not
recognize the faces—
crowds jeering at her…

        randi   saali   kutti
        daring to love
        an upper-caste boy

herself an out-
caste, Other. Out
side respectability.

        choochi   gaand   choot
        her broken body
        free for grabs.

When they are done,
her father will lead her
back to their hut,

        hand her a *sari*
        turn his head away
        so she can get dressed

 her hands shaking
as she tries to bind
together her bro ke n self.

V.

No Sita I was,
licked by fire—
your tongue

               but like Sita,
               subdued, dismissed,
               discarded

yet, still standing
my ground,
memories intact.

               I pack my bags,
               catch a plane
               back to my mother's.

Sita's sorry tale,
my sisters' blood,
and my own story

               light my pen on fire,
               which, like Hanuman—
               leaps and bounds

across the page,
burning, rewriting
the stories.

DEAR SITA

O daughter of the earth—
found in a furrow
embraced by folds of your mother's skin
you never forgot...

Did you immolate yourself in mud
to birth flowers and fruit,
morsels of your flesh
for your unborn children to savor,
remember your sacrifice?

Or, done with being dismissed, stolen,
                            and won,
did you choose to leave Ram
to return to your mother's house, Earth,
and your true passion—the land

to rebirth forests, rewrite the stories,
reclaiming body, seed, and soil.

BODY

OFFERING

for Lajja Savara

1940. You wear the red *sari* that will hang
in your cupboard for sixty-three years.

A veil of jasmine covers your eyes.
You try to recall your betrothed's face.

Clatter of silverware, loud laughter
shrouded in organza.

Girl cousins giggle behind shy smiles.
Boy cousins raise an inferno.

Seven lives, deaths knotted together—
follow him seven times around fire

with every *phera* losing
yet another layer of yourself

as student, daughter, friend.
Don't give up all of yourself,

your unborn daughters whisper
into your ear, but you ignore us

later that night, laying out
body, heart, and mind

across the four poster
ablaze with orange flowers.

HANDS LATTICED

with bridal *mehndi*,
she wore her weight in gold.
Her worth turned out much less.

She died that night,
was reborn a stranger
in her husband's house.

Learned his likes, dislikes,
forgot her own cravings
for *bhindi*, sun, and books.

Years later, womb emptied,
widowed, she struggled
to locate herself—

her mind, a noose
grasping at
empty coordinates.

PUTTAMA'S MIRACLE WASH

for Vidya Amberkar

Every day I rub into baby's skin—
brown bread dipped in milk.

She will become fair—one hundred percent—
brown bread dipped in milk.

What about you, dark-skinned Puttama,
you weren't dipped in milk?

Aiyo, back then, my mother
did not know such remedies.

GALINA—

with your short shorts,
cut-off to reveal half-moons

of your buttocks…
please forgive me
(when we were almost fifteen)

for telling you to cover up,
you were showing
too much and the boys

might see, might talk.
They did see, and you
saw that they saw

and the boys and you giggled
at your mutual pleasure—
reveling in your half-moons

peeping out of your shorts
just like your smile
slipping out of your mouth.

Forgive me, Galina,
covered and cowered
by false moralities

heaped upon by family,
school, the city at large,
but mostly by me—

the anvil of being judged
as lewd, a whore,
hanging above my head

I was too scared to step
outside the walls,
reframe my eyes to see

the world through your eyes—
moons and smiles,
whole and beautiful.

PORTRAIT

You are a *yakshi*, he says,
adorning the portals of Sanchi,
a *yogini,* spreading your legs
wide in *upavisthakona asana.*

I am just a girl, I giggle,
madly in love with your dimple,
your clumsy fingers so adroit
at drawing my portrait

which, I realized later, was all about you,
looked nothing like me.

PUNJABI WEDDING

This is my wedding, I will dance.
Laugh at me or join in—
I'll dance for all of us.

The singers: two boys, one man,
a large drum have arrived…
rhythms resonate through
our apartment's thin walls.
Soon, even strangers on the street below
snatch up the beat, *balle-balle*,
rub shoulders as they pass.

Women—bring out your once-in-a-lifetime saris—
Paithanis, Benarsis, Maheshwaris—
too heavy for just any occasion.
Men—your finest *Sherwanis*,
children—your silk *lehengas* and miniature *Nehru* coats.
Bedeck the bare streets and walls with yards
of purple, pink, bright green, gold
saturated silks.

Priests chant blessings, make money,
chant more blessings, invoke
sun, wind, and stars in our favor
as we walk seven times around fire,
pacing out seven lifetimes together
as man and wife.

Seven lives it will be, my sweet.
I've already died once in this life
(a prior marriage gone sour)
before I found you—
I cling to you now stickier than death.
Let's get on the dance floor—
dance to our past, present,
                    and future lives
as husband and wife.

SUMMONS

Promenade Road, Bangalore

When the skies leaked and rain collected
in messy puddles in our driveway

first, tadpoles appeared—
small, slippery as sperm.

Then, tiny frogs, hunched and springy
as the elastic between our legs

hopped about, slithery-smooth,
dark, grainy-eyes shining.

Their bodies thrummed with throaty calls
and the woods behind the house

picked up their call—
low, aching sounds

reverberating off tree trunks,
urging us, young and feverish—

throw off our blankets,
step into the night.

AIR

for Virgina Woolf

When we argue, and you fix
on me your silicon stare,
I turn into a whisper in the air.

In the green bushes, black veneer,
deep folds of the mind's ferment—
I am everywhere!

Your computational flair
cannot compare, contrast, denote
the haze, momentary pulse of my being

that freezes your fingers'
incessant chatter, invites you
to get lost in my vast cosmos—

twin peaks, moist tunnels—
bedazzled by the splendor
of my dark sun.

THE OTHER WIDOWS

for Rima Kashyap

White-*saried* widows
wash away the red
from center partings of hair,
tied back to remove
all traces of color—
nothing as luscious
as a red sun soaking
in grey-black waters.
They love to speak
of detachment—
perversity of other widows
who forget duties to dead husbands,
in-laws, children. Instead,
they roam the city's
uncombed streets,
hair loose and undone,
perfumed bodies
draped in yards
of overflowing color.

WHORLS

for Ishwar Parulkar

The flower within me unfolds
with the radiance
of your sun.

*

I cannot bear it when sleep separates us,
bodies touching but our minds—
wanton wanderers.

*

Life after life, your eyes steer us
through the whimsical
waters of time.

*

Suns are soaked
in my thirst
for you.

BELOVED MUMTAZ

Taj Mahal, Agra, India.
An ode from Shah Jahan, Emperor of India,
to his dead wife, Mumtaz Mahal

The translucence of white marble, your porous breathing
skin. Slender minarets, like your arms that embraced me
in love. The unbearable beauty of the universe distilled
in every inch of your body. You are alive, will live forever,
ivory hue changing with your many moods—aglow and
laughing with the flickering light of the late evening sun,
dark and gloomy under crying clouds, serene and radiant
under the full moon. Looming above manicured gardens
blooming with tulips, orchids, and lilies—sheer white,
magnificent—my beloved queen! Love brimming over the
arcs of perfect geometry.

BODY II:
THE CITY IS CLAIMED

SUNDAY AFTERNOON STROLL

Richmond Town, Bangalore

We slip on shards, pavements heaped
with broken bricks, garbage, a sleeping dog.
Men loiter around the sidewalk *chai* shop,
drinking *chai.* They stop their chatter
to stare at us. We step off the sidewalk
to bypass them, but narrowly miss
being hit by a cricket ball
thrown by boys playing on the road.

Ahead, a vagrant blocks our path.
We cross the road to avoid him.
I distract my six-year-old daughter,
pray she does not see him—
his hands, buried inside torn pant pockets,
waving with his penis.

Where are the girls?
my daughter wants to know.
She looks up at the surrounding
apartment buildings, wonders aloud
if the girls might be watching us
and the world go by
from window-slits cut out
from bare, blank-faced walls.

RAILWAY STATION

The train screeches to a halt at the station. The railway tracks, laid by farmers forced to abandon parched fields, gleam like lazy snakes basking in the sun. My American boyfriend stands at the doorway of our train's compartment. The station bell clangs, and just as the train begins to pull away, his bandana falls into the crack between the platform and the train. He reaches for it, ignoring my screams. As the train picks up speed, the tracks turn into snarling swords, wielded by thousands of invisible hands, gnashing at him.

THE PAINTED LADY

Kathmandu, Nepal

The innkeeper ushers us inside
his eighty-rupee a night guest house
in the center of old Kathmandu.

Through a cramped corridor, short doorway
with a carved wood engraving,
up narrow staircases

into a small bedroom. He opens
the window to a glimpse
of the golden pagoda.

Her hair is piled up in a spire,
single breast adorned with orange flowers.
Kohl-heavy eyes return our stare.

The innkeeper shuts the window,
turns to face us, his smile gold-toothed:
  "You want?"

THE DOLL

A child finds her amidst
broken bottles, used sanitary napkins,
dinner party scraps…
all dumped upon the sidewalk.

Still warm, her skin smells sweet
like apples just fallen, petal-soft lips
never creased in smile or frown,
closed eyes that never beheld the world.

She picks up and hugs the parched body,
tiny hands clenched in a tight fist.
Opens the fingers one by one—
wills them to bloom.

THE MIRROR
for Oscar Wilde

Give me gossip, the aunt said,
lying next to her niece,
afternoon sun drizzling diamonds
on the faded bedspread.

Her niece obliged:
As a child, father's body barely cold,
his brother (and yours)
moved nightly into my bed.

In the mirror, the aunt sees
her niece's bleeding eyes,
but then her own brother's face
appears. He didn't look

like himself though—
his beloved smile, a mere smirk,
creeping through the cracks,
the mirror's glass broken.

The aunt stands up, leaves the room:
Surely, you must be mistaken!
She pauses only to adjust the mirror—
glass intact again. Shining.

HIJRA AT THE INTERSECTION
for Kamala Das

She snakes her way
past rows of cars
at the intersection,
traffic stalled in both directions
at the blinking traffic light.
She purses her lips,
bangs her palms,
demands cash.
Once, held in esteem
for her blessings,
showered with money and gifts,
today, she is mocked
as if she were a freak,
drivers and passengers alike
rolling up windows in her face.

A resounding clap—
the skies break open.
Black streams of *kajal*
run down her face,
flat bosom bejeweled
with gaudy necklaces.
Her hair glistens
like wet tar on either side
of her chest. She cuts across
to the road-divide,
stands on it as if on a pedestal

herself a crossroad,
wilderness that wanders
between lines.
Hands burning red
constellations of fire,
she lifts up her skirt,
dances bawdily,
scorching onlookers
with the *darshan*
of her sawed-off stump,
hurtling a curse of barrenness
in a barren land,
shorn of animals and trees,
only seas of people,
motorcycles, autos, and cars—
honks blaring
at the broken lights.

CROCODILE LAKE REVISITED

for Sylvia Plath

You never had a chance
To show him your love—
Your father who hit you
With the hockey stick
You stole, hit you
In that dark closet for every
Goal you would go on
To score, called you:
Failure, worthless fool,
Never amount to much.
He died before
You could give it back,
Close the closet door—
Gaping hole where love
Ought to have grown.

At his funeral pyre,
You broke open his skull
With a stick
As you were told to do
As the eldest son.
And you did, but with
Vengeance, not fidelity
Or love, sent him off

To haunt ghouls
Instead of kids like you
In the spirit world.
Years later, fortune made,
No need to take any boy
Who doesn't bow down,
Has the better bike,
Down to Crocodile Lake,
Defy him to jump
Into jaw-infested waters.
Now you lure
With gold-flecked eyes,
Crocodile grin,
Sweet crooked words
As you bring any man
Unfortunate enough
To cross your lair
Into that same dark closet
Where your father beat you.
Offer him a drink or two,
You've already drunk
Too much yourself,
Enough to start
Your ritual taunt,
Haunts from your father.
First chip away
At your prey's accomplishments.
Then, spit slurs on his naked,

Shivering body:
Failure, worthless fool,
Never amount to much.
If he resists, fights back,
More chance to let loose
More verbal abuse,
Your tongue the hockey stick,
His ego the ball:
Hammer hammer
Pound pound
Right into the ground.

THIS CITY IS CLAIMED

Bangalore, India

This city is claimed—
Stench of piss
Rising, hissing.
Men keep
The bus waiting.
Unzip, sprinkle
Blessing upon soil
Concrete, tile,
Street corners,
Bus wheels, bushes,
Stretches of wall
Painted over with
Benevolent gazes—
Jesus, Ram,
A star and crescent.

No place for girls
In this city, odors
Of rancid male urine
Emanating from every
Public and private wall,
Nook and cranny
Hissing at them:
Stay away! Go home!
No raising of fingers:
One for *su-su*
Two for the *pu-pu*
No need to announce

The body's betrayal.
Valiant girls hold it in
Just a little longer
Cringing with pain.
The faint of heart
Slink away in shame
To the nearest W.C.

Grandmothers say
Girls have it good in the city.
Back in the village,
They must walk far out
Into distant fields in the dark,
Watch out for male avengers
Who might pounce.
Bodies spoken too loud,
Now free for grabs.
If they find a spot,
Check to make sure
No one is watching.
Then, squat down.
Release. Ah, the relief!
Streaming liquid gold.

After, hide the polluting
Evidence
Under mud or grass.
Wind your sari
Tight around your chest,
Stomach, hips.
Cover your head.
Body, a mummy—
Shut up!

SHAME

for all victims of honor killings

For years, I heard voices
inside my head
and outside, telling me
what to do, what to think—

Cross my legs, else—Shame!
Look a man in the eye—Shame!
My bloodied panties at thirteen
and every month thereafter—Shame!
Being born a woman—Shame!

Too much of her, and Shame
would swallow you alive
just like the ground opened up
to grab Sita:
Shame shame puppy shame
all the monkeys know your name

Married off at fourteen, molested
by my husband's brother
while my husband looked on.
Finally, I had enough.

Chalo, I thought, let's meet Shame.
I ran away with my childhood sweetheart.
My mother always said I'd watched
too many Bollywood movies:
Mere sapno ki rani kab ayegi tu

I knew what my own family
would do to me—*maar dalenge log mujhe.*
My brother found us, severed my head
from my body, carried it blood dripping…

all the way to the local police station,
handed himself over, along with my head.
A hero, they called him, for redeeming
our family's honor, rescuing me from the Devil.

But they didn't know—I myself
had invited the Devil into my arms,
along with my lover,
embraced her—my beloved Shame.

I'd tell anyone and everyone
how Shame had lain shivering
between our naked bodies,
kept warm by fires erupting

on our skins when we touched.
Small at first, the flames turned
into an inferno, engulfing us.
We died again and again   in bliss.

DEVIL'S DAUGHTERS

for Mirra Savara

Siberia does not seem far removed
as I read my daughter a well-traveled tale
of a plant who morphed into a maiden,
translucent skin revealing river veins.

The Devil's daughter murdered her.
She pasted the maiden's face onto
her own face, wreaking drought
on hapless crops, total devastation.

The village elders, brought in,
tied the Devil's daughter to four horses,
tore her limbs apart, buried her
dismembered parts in four distant corners.

Hearing the story's end, my daughter
shudders with fear, suddenly subdued.
Let out again, the village elders shriek
their sermons at her. She hears them

everywhere...in hoardings with women
peddling stoves and washing machines;
in her neighbors' kindly advice—a good girl
must not talk too much, laugh too loud.

If she does— the Devil 's daughter
will get her too. Then, the village elders,
along with men and bratty boys,
will come for her with sticks and slurs,

parade her naked around the village,
post her naked pictures online, brand her a slut—
drive the Devil out of her, leaving her
more dead than alive—a maiden.

CITY OF WIDOWS

Vrindavan, India

Waves of white wash over temple courtyards
in the city of the blue god.

No hint of color, no scent of jasmine,
tinkle of bells tracing light footsteps.
No longer wife, mother, or daughter,
even their names erased, changed
to the sound of a lone calf's cry: *Mai.*

To learn now how to live like a shadow—
no spark for love or life,
no yearning—save for Krishna!

Dear Krishna, true husband who never dies,
if Radha could not withstand your gaze,
what hope for pitiful widows yearning
to be your bride?

Once the widows arrive in Vrindavan,
there's no turning back, no looking
to see what they left behind.
They have to keep walking!
In Krishna's city of love and life,
they are the dead, still living,
hanging over the city like shrouds,
voices rising in songs

in praise of Krishna,
songs to keep their own bad luck at bay,
cleanse them of their deadly sin—
being alive while their husbands are dead.

Bodies borrowed for just a few years longer,
they wait for the day to lie down
next to Krishna on their nuptial bed—
logs of fire—the river gurgling beside them,
sweet wind from Krishna's flute
rippling flames through skin and bone,
blazing hearts.

SEED

BLOOD, OIL & WATER

A re-envisioning of tirandukalyanam, a Kerala ritual celebrating the onset of menstruation.

The first drop of blood is golden.
The heat in the room, chamber
built outside the house to keep her
apart, is as terrible as the heat
in her body. Spasms of pain
rip her apart. She calls out
to her mother
but no one answers.
Impure. Cast out. Alone.

The thick incense of coconut oil
permeates every corner
of the room, casting shadows
that dance on the walls.
Bhagirathi dances along, seizing
the girl's body as she destroys
the seeds of a universe,
washes away the ruins—
seed, sloughed off skin—with blood.
The girl is Bhagirathi.
Ferocious. All-powerful.

Deluge over, the girl's face
blooms like the tender
coconut flowers in the room.

Soon, her *amma* brings her sweet rice,
fresh soil for her womb.
Together, they walk to the lotus pond,
take a bath along with aunts,
older girl cousins, grandmothers—
breasts bobbing, loose and free,
hair fanned around them like dark flames.

Glistening with the water's sheen,
shimmering in new *saris*, they walk
past boys and men who stare at them
from the side of the road
unable to stop them
as they head straight for the temple,
break down locked doors,
stand fearless and unashamed
before their gods—their own divinity
stamped in red
between their thighs.

CONCRETE

Seventh grade, Bombay
for Meena and Gayatri

I hide my shame, red smear on my school uniform,
cowering between my best friends as they walk me to the
bathroom. The corridor closes in. *You have your chums,*
silly, says Meena after I confide that I am going to die. They
wash out the stain, giggling about which of the boys might
have seen it. My friends leave shortly after to join the rest
of the class playing basketball in the concrete courtyard.
I wait for my dress to dry. When I get home, my mother
will give me more sanitary napkins and a painkiller, then
turn away, not knowing what to say. I hear cheering and
laughter outside. I can't wait to join them. Forget this ever
happened.

FIRST TRIMESTER

for Sarah Bardeen

Vines crawl over the dining table,
tendrils bursting into leaves,

wide and green with expectation.
Tomorrow brings fresh surprises—

a hare's nose twitching behind
the television, bees brewing

honey on ceilings still moist
from the rains. My legs and arms

burgeon shoots, sprouted seed within—
warm and nested.

FRUITS

1.

Santra (orange)

Juice-laden
tendrils burst inside
the warm womb in my mouth—
sweet and sticky.

2.

Anjeer (fig)

Figs
hang
like testicles
on bare branches,
flowers blooming inside—
a profusion of exploding
stars.

3.

Aam (mango)

Curved
   like a woman,
      the mango kissed
       her lips. A passerby
        watched her eat amorously.
        He sucked the sweetness
       from her nipples, bored
      his tongues deep within.
      His licks sparked
     flames within her.
    When they cooled,
  a seed dropped—
 ripe and round.

RAIN DANCE

for Ishika & Anika

1.
Potter

Your eyes met mine—
we drifted back to land
bearing seed.

*

We poured ourselves
into a new mold in my body—
our baby girl.

*

Your face against my womb,
sweet fruit lying within—
cheek to cheek to cheek.

2.
Spring

Who can be melancholy
when spring visits our body,
new life blooms?

*

Streets are no longer lonely.
Shopkeepers, harried pedestrians,
neighbors we never knew before
stop. Smile. Baby talk.

Flowers bloom on concrete,
perfumes linger—two hearts
in my body pump so much love—
the world turns fair.

3.
Woman

Sweet companions—
we go together
into the same mysterious.

*

Our bodies morph and sway
in open seas—
clutch on!

*

Beaten into subjugation
what we should wear and weigh
how we should behave...
today, our bodies roar back—
huge and magnificent.

*

Women—run with the waves
towards the calling shore,
flow down with the rains,
bloom fruits and flowers.

*

Our stomachs expand
beyond all boundaries—
the formless, uncharted shape of love.

*

Womb—a vessel bequeathed
by my ancestor mothers.
My turn to fill it now.

4.
Pain

You rise
multi-hued, magnificent—
I have bowed before lesser gods.

5.
Drum

The skin upon my stomach
stretched thin and taut—
a drum on which you thump
with tiny feet: *I'm here! I'm here!*

6.
Geometry

Sum of our parts
whole from our halves—
you make us complete.

*

Your body curls within
arc within arc—
together we encircle the universe.

*

From undulating curves
life arises—
a full circle.

7.
Journey

A cosmos balloons within me.
I can do nothing
but let go—

*

You travel in orbits
set in motion by the distant
glimmer of stars.

8.
Baby Krishna

Blood of my blood,
breath of my breath,
I cannot tell us apart.

*

Who can stop this falling
out of known worlds?
Who can stop this falling
in love with you?

*

You claim my food,
my very breath—
devour me!

9.
Oceans

Sleep, little baby
deep within your liquid world,
sleep until ready to swim ashore.

10.
Words

This twilight hour
between sleep and waking
births words on the molten page.

SLEEP SONATA

Months of tidal urges in your ocean womb
you've started to forget
(even as you remember more)
the fog of memory settling in your mind
since you got ashore.

Your mind, a giant weed, creeps in
brick by brick to help you adjust
to our mortar world. Soon,
you tire and crumble, dissolving
into fitful cries, shrieks, and howls,
demanding to be held, taken back to sea.

I take you down to the seashore…
a quiet book, lights off,
wait for the tide to drag you
back to your ocean home
Take rest there, be soothed
by the steady rhythm, sway of waves,
stay until sea winds wash you
back to shore, and you awake.

THE FIRST YEAR

She winds around the house
collecting dust, picking up toys,

pieces of herself. Keeps march-time
to the laundry drum, kettle's whistle.

Too many gaping mouths—the stove's fire,
her baby's howl that tears

a hole in her heart. She falls inside,
is unable to get out—

captive to her baby's eyes,
slave to her baby's cries.

ORBIT

for Tanu Mehrotra Wakefield

You whir around the house, poking holes
in the shelves, closets, clean floor.

Home destroyed, you demand to be held
just as we walk out of the door.

I resign. Baby Krishna ate dirt
but when his mother opened his mouth

to wash it out, she saw the universe inside—
planets, stars, entire galaxies

exploding.
Expanding—

PUBERTY

for Ishika Parulkar

At the edge of the world,
our daughter swings between
spitting abuse at us and her younger sister,
then skulking back for a quick hug,
snuggling on our laps to bounce
her childhood back into herself again.
Idiot, she calls us, *Fart. Faaaarrrrt.*
She loves how it sounds, revels
in hurtling the word at us
as if it were a glob of shit.
She wants to demean, obliterate us,
and with us, the child that still lurks in her.
With each utterance, she spreads
nascent wings that bud upon her thin back,
flutters them as she takes a small hop and skip
towards the cliff from where, one day,
she hopes to jump off—
soar away by herself, unfettered.

SOIL

EVOLUTION

for Krithi Karanth

Anchored
by hands and feet
to the ground,
my baby's spine dips
and arcs like a bird.

She noses ahead
of the sniffing dog
for the morsel
nestled in carpet folds—
the taste of conquest.

One day, enticed
by the table top,
she stands up,
her senses high above
the ground.

Slowly, the jungle recedes,
condemning her
to wander
for the rest of her life—
searching for lost scents.

BACK TO THE WOMB

Backyard gardens remind the babies in us
of our mother's wombs—

trickle from the tap—heartbeat
rustle of grass—blood river.

OMENS
Lalbagh Gardens, Bangalore

I.
Under the turquoise sky, I see
a cobra flare its fluted head,
sprint a sideways dance towards us
on emerald lawns.

The cobra turns away to the right
just before reaching us—
my unborn baby and me—
prodded along by five jet black crows.

Our ancestors, in the form of crows,
come to protect us from danger.
An ancient rhyme counting crows
decodes the messages they send:

> *One for sorrow, two for joy,*
> *three for a lover, four for a boy*
> *five for a miss…*

what's there to miss?

II.
Weeks pass. Venomous snakes—
superbugs writhing on the hospital's
gleaming walls—bite us. A narrow miss,
but my newborn baby and I survive.

A dream of a white elephant
foretold the birth of the Buddha…
what of the black-winged crows,
glint in the snake's eye?

I stare outside the hospital's prison walls
for another sign, but this time
both sky and ground are clear—
cobra and crows gone.

THE TOY ROOM

Velvet snails leave trails of thread,
fluorescent frogs, plastic hippopotami
stare beady-eyed. Monkeys hang
from curtain rods, macaws screech out
taped calls—cries for help
as their wild counterparts disappear
from lost jungles
to reappear in the toy room...
tooth and claw gone,
good to be squeezed and hugged,
return our affections with painted smiles.

TATIANA

San Francisco Zoo, December 25, 2007
for Ulhas Karanth

No shrine, this cage,
pedestal of fake rock—
a throne from where she is
displayed to the world.

Once revered in the jungle,
visitors to the zoo
throw stones, jeer as she paces
by barbed wire.

A fortress separates them; yet
with determined eye, she clears
the wall of her enclosure
with an astounding leap—

predator once again after being prey,
she stalks her three tormentors...
severs the neck vein of one,
chases after the other two

with each step, regaining
lost grandeur, stripes sizzling fire—
> *Tyger tyger burning bright,*
> *In the forest of the night*

Then, zoo rangers shoot her dead.
Lying in regal repose,
she reclaims her right to die—
out in the open.

M.S. ATTACK

for Anuradha Sahni

I.

Child in a woman's body, you crawl furiously
to get outside the confines of your hospital room,
your mind that binds you to this moment
that is not you. Threads fraying, memories
unshackled, you catch them one by one—
the fire that burnt your finger, chasing
purple-pink butterflies, velvet-smooth crayons,
silky sheen of the dress that hugged
your curves at your high school dance—
the most beautiful girl in the room.
The stream of specialists needed now
to show you how to put one foot
before the next to walk, take a shower,
2+2=4, not 1972, the year you were born.
You've learned all this before, but answers
float away like balloons, threads too short to catch.

II.

Your desire to fashion space, rebuild your childhood
is put on hold. No longer can you clear the paths,
your childhood home filled with moldy newspapers,
furniture, empty bottles and tins—
accumulated over years by your mother,
seeking to calm the chaos in her mind,
but adding only clutter and more clutter.
You only wished for space and light
but how to bring it inside the womb?
Now, behind drawn curtains, you dissect
endless highways of nerves colliding

in jumbled pools, piles of clutter
in your own mind, arrested motion
un-mapping your vision and world.
Form to formlessness—the world turns blind.
You wonder what Nietzche would have said.

III.
 You loved to mold your body
into cosmic geometries—
Trikonasana, Adhomokhasvanasana.
Loved to absorb the ocean's ebb and flow
with your breath, taste life from all orifices—
your eyes, nose, mouth, vagina, ass.
New life you will never grow as nerves lie strangled.
Your DJ mind spins traces of colors and sounds.
Meaning dammed in bloodless pools.

IV.
Ancient paths usurped by new gods:
Cytoxan, Rebiff, Avonex, Copaxone.
A rainbow of pills, the new gods' gifts,
now mark the hours—blues for morning,
pinks for afternoon, yellow for night.
White-robed guardians extract penance:
nausea, depression, a liver perhaps, no desire
save to kill yourself—the price to pay
for an extra day alive. Your body forgot
its original path, and you are blind
without maps, scalpels, stethoscopes, MRIs—
only the new gods have directions.

V.

Stubborn child, you refuse to accept
your body's transgression.
No more dictates from new gods!
Call forth ancient mediators!
From village farm to the city
bring roots, leaves, bark, berries—
recall celestial music, revive sleeping rhythms,
restore the flow of life back
in the way of stars.
Hear me liver! Hear me body!
Hear me Kali, hear me Durga,
my own sleeping mother—
wake up! Let me live.

THE LEELA POEMS
for Leela Raut

I.

Independence Day
15th August, Lalbagh, Bangalore

After four days, the train spills them
into the station, these farmers,
forced to flee their barren fields,
mud still inside their nails and blood.
In the city, crowded into crannies,
they sweep other people's dust
that needs no watering to grow,
peel and chop fruits and vegetables
cut off long since from the stalk.
Once, open fields joined them
to the sky and each other. Now,
walls, separate plates and mugs
keep them apart. Still,
once a year, on Independence Day,
they meet up at Lalbagh—
coalescing from all over the city,
to chat, eat roasted *bhutta*,
stand tall as the trees
bare feet caressing red earth.

2.
Boats

Leela cries softly over
her husband's sores
from standing all night
waiting on others.

She caresses his bruised body
both their frailties
held together intact
by her shaking frame.

Her mistress wishes
she too could burst
into sobs or laughter,
catch others within

her waves, carry them
over to her shore.
But her mind will not
let her body break—

lest Leela sees,
lest Leela talks—
holding it up
with splinters, cast, and nails.

3.
Indulgence

Leela massages oil into her scalp,
glistening palms working
long, black tresses
like the floors she scrubs all day.

After, she washes with *shikakai,*
squats on the porch,
sun splashing over her face,
open meadow of hair.

5.
Blessings

I.
Tail end of a whip her spinal cord wields—
crazed ringmaster, drumming pain.

Alone in her hut, Leela slaps it silent.
Final heave, her body cleaves open.

She cuts the cord with a kitchen knife,
cradles her baby in smiling arms.

II.
I add Leela's story to my necklace,
each bead a birthing tale,
brought by mothers come to visit.

My own story: a cracked bead.
A hospital's operating theatre,
my spine, a sedated snake.

On the screen, I watch gloved masked men
pull out a baby from some woman's body—
but then they give the baby to me.

After—wombs of boils burgeon
on both my baby and my skin.
Doctors scalpel out pus and blood.

I want to rest, but my spine will not let me,
hissing and spitting, shooting venom.
Furious—baby taken without its blessing.

5.
Blood bond

Harvest time, with Leela busy in the fields,
Leela's neighbor nurses Leela's baby,

along with her own child, one on each breast—
turning milk back to blood.

6.
Badmaash

Badmaash girls in Leela's village,
married off early, are weighed down
with husband, house, and child,
leaving no time for *badmaash* ways.

One *badmaash* wife—run away
with her Muslim lover—
hunted down by villagers
with picket forks and knives.

The *badmaash* wife, her lover,
and cuckold husband—all killed,
lives unraveled from the village fabric
leaving only broken threads.

7.
Aai (mother)
for Madhavi Parulkar

Seeing Leela suffer our own food
made to suit our children's bland palates

Aai cooks for her—green chillies
fried in mustard oil and turmeric

morsels of tenderness Leela relishes
bridging the distance

between servant and master,
vast as the crossing to reach Sita.

8.

Lemon rice
Bangalore 2012

Shaken like a rattle for eating
lemon rice sprinkled with cashews
she'd cooked earlier in the day

the servant girl, scarcely fifteen,
jumps off the twelfth floor balcony,
falls on concrete below—

her body smooshed
to the consistency of boiled rice,
skew of bones like nuts.

9.

Leela's song

Carry us back
on the sun's rising rays
to our rice fields.

No longer tend
to marble floors, porcelain tubs
not ours to use.

Lonely no longer,
steady chatter of companions
sees us through

the long day. City money
in our pockets, we shoo away
crow money lenders.

Day after day, needle tufts of rice
into water and mud—
embroideries

to embellish the earth
that loves us back in return—
gifting rich harvests.

Carry us back
on the sun's rising rays
to our rice fields.

NOTES

(please also see foreword and glossary)

BELOVED MUMTAZ   Shah Jahan, the Mughal emperor of India, griefstricken when his favorite wife, Mumtaz Mahal died, built the Taj Mahal in Agra, India to honor her memory. Both Mumtaz Mahal and he are buried there.

BLOOD, OIL & WATER   In Kerala, and other parts of India, menstruating girls and women are kept separate from others in the house as they are considered to be polluting. They are also not allowed to enter temples during this period.

CITY OF WIDOWS   Another name for Vrindavan, a city in India that is home to many Hindu widows and is also considered the birthplace of Krishna. Widows who are forced out of their homes go to Vrindavan where they spend most of their time singing *bhajans,* or devotional songs, to Krishna.

CROCODILE LAKE REVISITED   According to Hindu custom, when a father dies, the eldest son is expected to release his father's spirit for his next life by breaking his father's skull on his funeral pyre.

FIRE TRIALS   The title refers to the trials that Sita undertook to prove her purity.

OFFERING   During Hindu marriage ceremonies, the girl follows her future husband seven times around a fire.

PUNJABI WEDDING   Hindus believe in reincarnation. They could have the same partners they have in their current lives in past and future lives.

SHAME   Women who break social norms are the target of "honor" killings whereby a family member might kill the woman to save the honor of the family.

THE CITY IS CLAIMED   It is common to see men urinating in public in India whereas girls/women have to be discrete about going to the bathroom. In the city, they often have to wait until they return home; villagers have to go the bathroom far out in the fields.

THE LEELA POEMS   Hundreds of villagers and farmers move to cities to work as domestic live-in help. Depending on where they work, they might have to eat and drink out of separate dishes, and eat only after everyone else has eaten.

THE OTHER WIDOWS   Hindu widows traditionally renounce all color and dress only in white.

GLOSSARY

Aai: mother

Aam: mango

Aiyo: exclamation akin to "Oh dear!"

Amma: mother

Anjeer: fig

Adhomokhasvanasana: yoga pose

Badmaash: rascal

Bahu: daughter-in-law

Balle–balle: Punjabi phrase similar to "hurrah." It is used while dancing to keep the beat

Bhagirathi: also, known as Shakti, a female goddess who destroys evil spirits

Bhindi: okra

Bhutta: corn on the cob

Chai: Indian tea made with milk and spices

Chakra: round firecracker used during Diwali

Chochli: breast

Choot: cunt

Darshan: viewing of god or a holy person

Dharma: life purpose/ duty in Hinduism

Diya: Indian oil lamps. Traditionally made of clay, they are lit during Diwali and other auspicious occasions.

Durga: fierce form of the mother goddess

Hanuman: monkey God worshipped by Hindus. Ram's greatest devotee, he helped Ram by finding Sita.

Hijra: (in South Asia) a person whose birth sex is male but who identifies as female or as neither male nor female (Oxford English Dictionary). Historical: a eunuch

Gaand: buttocks, ass

Ganesha: an elephant-headed god worshipped by Hindus often at the start of endeavors as he is said to be the *"remover of obstacles."*

Junglee: wild

Kajal, kohl: black powder used in South Asia as an eyeliner or as a mark on the forehead

Kali: Hindu goddess of time, creation, destruction, and power

Lakshman: brother of Ram in the epic *Ramayana.*

Lunds: penises; lund: penis

Lehengas: a full ankle-length skirt worn by Indian women

Mai: mother

Mehndi: paste derived from an Indian bush applied decoratively to the hands often in marriage ceremonies

Maar dalenge log mujhe: people will kill me

Mere sapno ki rani kabhi ayegi tu: a popular Hindi song meaning "When will you come, O queen of my dreams"

Nehru: hip-length formal Indian coat buttoned to the top with a mandarin collar, named after the former Prime Minister, Pundit Nehru

Pallav: the end part of the sari that is thrown over the shoulder. It is generally the decorative part of the sari.

Pati-dev: husband-god; treating the husband like a god

Phera: going around a sacred fire. During a Hindu marriage ceremony, a couple takes seven rounds or *pheras* around the sacred fire.

Phulkas: Indian flat bread made of ground wheat

Pu pu: Punjabi word for faeces

Radha: consort of Krishna

Rakshasi: demoness

Ram: crown prince and then king of Ayodhya. Main character in the epic, *Ramayana.* He is an *avatar,* or bodily manifestation, of the great Hindu god, Vishnu, and is worshipped as a god by Hindus.

Randi: whore

Ravan: king of Lanka (from the epic *Ramayana)*

Santra: orange (fruit)

Sari: garment from the Indian subcontinent that consists of a drape five to nine yards long.

Sherwani: formal Indian knee-length coat buttoned to the neck

Shikakai: herb used as shampoo

Sita: wife of Ram, daughter of the goddess Earth.

Shurpanakha: demoness who tried to seduce Ram and Lakshman. Lakshman cut off her nose when she attacked Sita out of jealousy.

Swayamvara: a practice in ancient India whereby a girl, most often royalty chose a husband publicly from a list of suitors.

Trikonasana: yoga pose

Upavisthakona asana: yoga pose

Valmiki: author of the *Ramayana*

Vrindavan: birth place of Krishna. Hindu widows go to Vrindavan when they are forced out of their homes in India.

Yakshi: female earth spirit in Hindu and Buddhist mythology

Yogini: female practitioner of yoga

Athena Kashyap grew up in Bangalore and Bombay, and attended college, both undergraduate and graduate, in the United States. Her first book, *Crossing Black Waters,* was published by Stephen F. Austin State University Press, Texas in 2012. Her poetry has been published in *Exquisite Corpse, Prairie Schooner, The Fourth River* among other journals and has been anthologized in the U.S., England, and India. She currently lives in San Francisco, CA where she teaches English at City College of San Francisco.